MW00427233

Tai Chi for Beginners

Find Serenity and Inner Peace through the Ancient Art of Tai Chi

(Tai Chi Chuan | Taijiquan)

by Miao Ri Lemahieu

Table of Contents

Introduction 1

Chapter 1: Understanding Tai Chi Chuan (Taijiquan) and the Four Core Disciplines 5

Chapter 2: The 10 Vital Points of Tai Chi Chuan 11

Chapter 3: Benefits of Tai Chi 15

Chapter 4: Tai Chi Exercises for Beginners 21

Chapter 5: How to Find Serenity and Inner Peace through Tai Chi in 10 Steps 29

Chapter 6: 18 Important Tips for Practicing Tai Chi 35

Conclusion 41

Introduction

Do you find it hard to relax after a hard day's work at the office? Do you spend sleepless nights feeling anxious about what will happen the following day? Do you explode in fury at the slightest provocation? Does your body feel tired and spent even during the middle of the day? If you have answered "yes" to any of these questions, you may be a person who is in need of the revitalization and positive energy that Tai Chi can provide.

Tai Chi is a form of Chinese martial arts that is more like a dance or an exercise. It has been shown to promote body and mind capabilities by enhancing a person's stamina, strengthening the body and boosting overall mental capacities. This in turn allows you to have a better life that is harmonious with the forces around yourself. There are plenty more benefits that you can obtain from Tai Chi, which will be presented in Chapter 3 of this book.

Prepare yourself to be absolutely amazed at how purposeful this ancient form of Chinese martial art is. This book is designed to present the basic movements you'll need to learn, amongst the many hundreds of Tai Chi techniques. It will also teach you how to find serenity and inner peace through the practice of Tai Chi. Continue reading to learn about why Tai Chi has become so staggeringly popular throughout the world.

© Copyright 2014 by LCPublifish LLC - All rights reserved.

This document is geared towards providing reliable information in regards to the topic and issue covered. The publication is sold with the idea that the publisher is not required to render accounting, officially permitted, or otherwise, qualified services. If advice is necessary, legal or professional, a practiced individual in the profession should be ordered.

- From a Declaration of Principles which was accepted and approved equally by a Committee of the American Bar Association and a Committee of Publishers and Associations.

In no way is it legal to reproduce, duplicate, or transmit any part of this document in either electronic means or in printed format. Recording of this publication is strictly prohibited and any storage of this document is not allowed unless with written permission from the publisher. All rights reserved.

The information provided herein is stated to be truthful and consistent, in that any liability, in terms of inattention or otherwise, by any usage or abuse of any policies, processes, or directions contained within is solely and completely the responsibility of the recipient reader. Under no circumstances will any legal responsibility or blame be held against the publisher for any reparation, damages, or monetary loss due to the information herein, either directly or indirectly.

Respective authors own all copyrights not held by the publisher.

The information herein is offered for informational purposes solely, and is universal as so. The presentation of the information is without contract or any type of guarantee assurance.

The trademarks that are used are without any consent, and the publication of the trademark is without permission or backing by the trademark owner. All trademarks and brands within this book are for clarifying purposes only and are the owned by the owners themselves, not affiliated with this document.

Chapter 1: Understanding Tai Chi Chuan (Taijiquan) and the Four Core Disciplines

Tai Chi has a string of purposes. Various teachers have different goals when using Tai Chi. Some teachers use it to reconcile the body and the mind, while others may use it for self-defense. Whatever the reason, the ultimate goal of Tai Chi is always beneficial to the person practicing it- beneficial to the mind, body and spirit.

What is Tai Chi Chuan?

Tai Chi Chuan or Taijiquan is a type of martial arts that originated from China and was created by Taoists. Tai Chi Chuan is literally translated as Tai ("the great") and Chi ("everywhere") and Chuan ("way"). Its purpose is developing harmony in both the internal and external aspects of your consciousness. It intends to create congruence between your mind, body and spirit; and between you and the universe (Tao).

Taoists believe that for one to stay healthy and rejuvenated, they should develop, store and use their Chi, or life energy. Chi is also the basis of acupuncture that is now widely accepted in the West as an alternative form of treatment. The meridians in which Tao Chi is based are also the meridians for acupuncture. This indicates that Tao Chi has a scientific basis, and is indeed an effective method.

Although it is a self-defense method, you do not need physical strength to practice it effectively. Instead, you need your inner strength to be able to perform Tai Chi workouts. Incredibly enough, you can counter a major punch successfully by using Tai Chi; and with less physical energy.

Furthermore, it is considered a form of exercise to revitalize your body, and promote health and fitness. Your internal organs are also massaged during the process, allowing rejuvenation of body cells.

In addition, Tai Chi is believed to unlock the power of Qi (energy force), and balance the Yin and the Yang (two opposite but complementary forces) in the body. Examples of Yin (dark) and Yang (sunny) are: male and female; sunny and dark, liquid and solid, short and tall, and north and south.

The four core disciplines of Tai Chi/Chuan

There are four core disciplines of Tai Chi Chuan and these are:

1. Taoist Meditation

This is a type of meditation that involves the development of a peaceful and empty mind. Before the meditation, stretches are done, followed by silent meditation. If a teacher is conducting the meditation, Taoist beliefs are introduced before and after the meditation. At times, healing sounds are introduced as well, to promote focus.

2. Yang short and long Tai Chi form

This discipline is considered a special class, because it includes the powerful self-defense techniques that Tai Chi practitioners do. The short form is practiced before the more complex long form.

3. Eternal Spring Chi Kung

This discipline was created by Master C.K. Chu, and it involves a healing exercise program in which breathing techniques are coordinated with the exercises.

4. Advanced level training

This involves advanced, high level fighting forms with the use of weapons. You can proceed to this level if you plan to use Tai Chi as a means of self-defense. If not, the movements are enough to allow you to succeed in life, while staying healthy at the same time.

A combination of the different techniques is utilized by experts who know how to mix and match the various forms and movements.

There are four Tai Chi styles namely:

1. **Yang** – This is the most widely used Tai Chi form nowadays.

2. **Hao** – This is the least practiced among the Tao Chi forms.

3. **Chen** – This is practiced by advance Tao Chi practitioners because it's more difficult than the rest of the techniques.

4. **Wu** – This is a modification of the Yang technique. It is usually utilized by beginners.

Chapter 2: The 10 Vital Points of Tai Chi Chuan

There are 10 vital points for Tai Chi Chuan, and these are:

1. **There must be harmony of the internal and the external.** This is the end goal of Tai Chi. When this happens, your health and your life improve, and you will have more success in your endeavors.

2. **There should also be harmony of the lower and upper body.** Before you can establish harmony with the external forces, you must first develop unity within yourself. You can achieve this through constant Tai Chi workouts.

3. **There must be fluidity and continuity of movement.** Any interruption in your moves will cause disruption of the Chi or energy passing through your body. Keep this in mind.

4. **The elbows are usually down and the shoulders are relaxed.** The original positions of the exercises are these, so take note of them.

5. **The waist must also be relaxed.** This area is important for the energy to pass through without breaking. The energy cannot do this if this portion is

tense. The Chi energy is likened to an ocean the water cannot be segmented into waves or lakes. The energy has to be whole to be effective.

6. **Your mental strength, not your physical strength, must be used**. This is also important to remember. You are not having a contest to determine who is physically strongest. You are trying to develop your mental strength and internal strength.

7. **Your chest should be relaxed and your back should be raised**. Likewise, your waist should be relaxed together with your waist for the Tai Chi to be effective.

8. **You must be able to distinguish what's full and what's empty.** As you progress slowly with your Tai Chi workouts, you will have no trouble determining whether you are full or empty. This is in terms of energy and strength.

9. **The energy emanating from your head must be sensitive and light**. One major source of energy is the head. You have to visualize accurately so that the energy that emanates from your head is sensitive and light.

10. **Find serenity in your movements.** Tai Chi is meditation in motion, so learn how to find peace and

calm while performing your continuous movements or Tai Chi exercises.

Different styles have emerged from a number of different teachers. They have each devised modifications to the Tai Chi workouts or exercises. These are all effective, but the most common is the Yang moves or Tai Chi Chuan forms. Practice at home, and save yourself from stress and unhealthy conditions.

Chapter 3: Benefits of Tai Chi

Tai Chi has the major goal of harmonizing your mind, body and soul. It can also help you to unify yourself with the forces of the universe. Seems like a superhero requirement, but it is true. You can reach your maximum potential if you practice Tai Chi religiously. Sometimes called the "ultimate fist", there are various benefits to Tai Chi that you can reap - especially if you proceed to its higher form. The benefits are listed below:

1. **Reduces stress** - It has been proven through the years that Tai Chi reduces stress and anxiety. The body movements are in congruence with the mind that is able to reduce your stress level. When stress is not managed properly, a number of illnesses can result, such as cardiovascular diseases and hypertension.

2. **Promotes sleep** – People who practiced Tai Chi were observed to have no sleeping problems. They sleep longer and more soundly than those who did not exercise.

3. **Enhances body coordination** - There is smooth coordination throughout the body, and body movements are flexible and fluid.

4. **Revitalizes internal organs** – Because of the Tai Chi movements, the internal organs are massaged

and revitalized. This prevents organ dysfunction, and promotes proper body function.

5. **Maintains bone density** - It is believed that Tai Chi maintains bone density in people who perform the techniques. It is because the bones are strengthened with the Tai Chi workouts.

6. **Relieves pain** – Tai Chi can also provide relief from pain. If you are experiencing pain due to muscle fatigue or some other existing pathologic condition, Tai Chi can be the natural "drug" of choice that can ease your pain.

7. **Improves blood circulation** – Your blood circulation improves. This facilitates the elimination of substances that can block proper blood flow. Absorption of nutrients from the bloodstream is maintained too.

8. **Strengthens immune system** - Your immune system becomes stronger because of proper body function. Cells such as your white blood cells (WBCs), and T-lymphocytes are produced sufficiently to counter foreign particles in your body.

9. **Develops self-defense techniques** – You will learn reliable self-defense techniques that you can apply whenever necessary.

10. **Improves balance of COPD patients** – Studies have proven that people with chronic obstructive pulmonary disease (COPD) have significantly improved their quality of life after Tai Chi exercises.

11. **Reduces the risk of arthritis** – Because of the Tai Chi movements, the risk of developing arthritis is reduced. Body joints are able to cooperate better with the whole body.

12. **Reduces high blood pressure** – The Tai Chi exercises have been proven to reduce high blood pressure and maintained normal blood pressure. This is due to the fact that blood circulation was improved.

13. **Helpful in recuperation of stroke patients** – Tai Chi exercises were found to be helpful in allowing stroke patients to become mobile again. Their mobility became better and the quality of their lives was enriched as a result.

14. **Helpful in breast cancer patients** – Tai Chi has helped breast cancer patients to improve the quality

of their lives, and allows them to function as normally as possible.

15. **Lowers risk of heart ailments** – A study found that patients practicing Tai Chi have lower risk of contracting heart attacks or myocardial infarctions, and strokes or cardiovascular attacks.

16. **Helps lower bad cholesterol and triglycerides** – Tai Chi has been proven to lower harmful fats in the body like cholesterol levels and triglycerides. The accumulation of these bad fats in your blood vessels can block them, which in turn can cause atherosclerosis, hypercholesterolemia and triglyceridemia.

17. **Improves lives of Parkinson patients** – Parkinson's disease patients who have undergone or are currently undergoing Tai Chi exercises demonstrated improved walking ability and physical activities.

18. **Strengthens muscles** – The muscles are strengthened and toned due to the inner and outer energy acquired through the exercise.

19. **Improves body flexibility** – Your body becomes more flexible because the techniques promote muscle fluidity.

20. **Improves balance** – You will have more control of your body because you can maintain your balance without any problems.

21. **Boosts mental abilities** – Due to the harmony of your mind, body and spirit, your mental abilities are developed and enhanced. You can think more clearly, focus easily and process knowledge promptly. Your memory, as well as your analytical skills, will most likely increase.

22. **Builds your self-confidence** – Your ability to cope with stress and your enhanced mental prowess will make you more self-confident in your life overall.

23. **Improves your quality of life in general** – This is due to the inner and outer harmony that occurs within yourself and your environment. When everything is in sync, your quality of life improves and you can succeed at anything you set out to do.

These are the excellent benefits you can gain from Tai Chi. So, let's roll up our sleeves and get started. Learn those Tai Chi workouts now and live a happy and successful life.

Chapter 4: Tai Chi Exercises for Beginners

Tai Chi beginners will have to learn the basic techniques first. Executing the process step-by-step will ensure your success at learning Tai Chi. The best way to go about this is to learn under a certified Tai Chi master- but with commitment and dedication, you can learn the basic techniques presented in this book.

Before undertaking any type of exercise, whether it is Tai Chi or not, you must first consult your doctor. You may have a condition where exercise is contraindicated. Only when your doctor gives you the go-ahead should you proceed. Wear comfortable, loose clothing and shoes to allow free body movements. You can start with a meditation, and then continue on to the exercises. You must also meditate while exercising.

There are several Tai Chi forms that are named after the masters who established them. All the exercises have these common characteristics: the feet should remain firmly planted on the ground, and movements should be light and fluid.

Beginners can be anyone who has not yet perfected the Tai Chi movements. You can do the exercises for years, yet still be considered a beginner. It is expected that you will not feel a powerful Qi or Chi during the first sessions of your Tai Chi. It might even take years for you to feel the power of your Chi, but you will definitely feel it eventually. So keep going!

21

Here are some Tai Chi exercises you can learn as a beginner.

1. Warm up exercises

Before doing Tai Chi exercises, you should always warm up. You can accomplish this by performing simple leg or arm stretches. You may also move your head from side to side or around your neck, and rock back and forth on your toes. Hip rotation with your arms hanging by your sides can also apply. Do these exercises for a few minutes until you feel ready to begin. Start with the short forms.

2. Hand exercises

Stand with your feet about one foot apart. Inhale and extend your arms in front of you with your palms down. They have to be in line with your shoulders. Exhale and rotate your wrists clockwise and then counter clockwise until you feel your arms loosen up.

You can also do the beak exercises (when you form a beak shape with your fingers by extending your arms and then joining your thumb and fingers and letting your fingers and wrist move downwards)

3. Windmill exercises

Stand up with your legs about two feet apart. Allow your hands to hang at your sides. Bring your hands together over your groin area with the fingers pointing downwards. Inhale deeply and slowly raise your hands over your head, this time with your fingers pointing upwards.

Allow your hands to rest for a few seconds over the chest area before proceeding over the head. With your arms above your head, exhale while arching your head upwards and your spine backwards. Lower your arms to your sides while gradually bending your head downwards. Return to your original position. You can do this several times while doing the breathing exercises. Remember that you must feel your muscles relax while performing these exercises.

4. Knee exercises

Place the fingers of each of your hands over each knee with the fingers pointing towards the center. Your feet must be at least a foot apart and pointed slightly inward. Rotate each knee upwards, left, downwards and then right. Do this at least 8 to 15 times.

5. Single Whip

The single whip can have variations based on the Tai Chi family style. The single whip is done by standing with your feet at least about two feet apart, and knees slightly bent. Raise both arms with the fingers of your right hand forming a beak and the left hand with the palm turned outwards. Return your arms to your sides and then raise your arms again. This is the Wu style. It's a good exercise in releasing stress and tension.

The Yang or Chuan version of the single whip has some modifications. Instead of facing front, you face slightly to the left with your left foot slightly forward. The same formation of the right hand remains, but the left hand is also positioned slightly more forward than the right hand.

6. Raising hands and lowering arms

Stand in a normal position: back straight, hands at your sides and feet together. Inhale and exhale deeply through the nose. Do this at least 8 to 10 times. Next, slow down your respiration by allowing 5 seconds to lapse before inhaling. Wait for 1 to 2 seconds before exhaling. Extend your exhalation longer than your inhalation for about 3 to 4 seconds.

Position your feet to ensure they are at least shoulder-width apart, and raise your arms slowly to shoulder level as you inhale. Return them to your sides as you exhale. Perform these exercises several times until you feel relaxed. You can close your eyes to visualize yourself relaxing.

7. Low kicks

The stance is done by standing with your legs apart and your knees slightly bent, as though preparing to spring. Your hands should both be raised with the palms open. Rock back and forth on your legs, and then balance yourself with one leg while extending the other leg to give a low kick.

8. Push hands

The simplest form of the push-hand exercises is the wrist-to-wrist form. This is done by a back to back wrist exercise with another person. Your left leg is a step forward from your right leg, and your left hand is against the other person's right hand. Your palms and wrists are back-to-back against each other. Your body is also inclined slightly forward towards the person. You can rock back and forth on your knees, while maintaining the wrist-to-wrist position.

You can also take a step or two forward and backward without disengaging from your contact point, which is the back of your hand and your wrist. In this position, there is an exchange of energies with your partner. This is one combat form of your Tai Chi Chuan.

9. Playing the Lute

Start with your left leg about one step forward, with your hands held high as though you are playing a lute (the musical instrument). Place your weight on your left leg, and then place your right foot behind your left foot about a half step away. Shift your weight to the center as though to sit on your right leg. Next, extend your left leg using your heels, while rotating your waist slowly to the right. Then raise your arm up to nose-level. Guard the inside of your left elbow by slightly lowering your right hand to protect your elbow.

10. Unfolding the arms like a fan

This one mimics the movement of fanning yourself. Inhale deeply, step down on your left heel, and raise your hands with both palms facing upwards. On the other hand, the right hand moves towards the left and then upwards above the head with the palms facing upwards. You can exhale while doing this. Shift the weight into your left leg and bow.

These are some simple exercises that you can adapt while doing breathing exercises and emptying your mind simultaneously. Be sure that your focus is on the mind and your internal state. There is no way to perform these workouts perfectly if you do not relax your mind and free the body of stress and tension.

Learning Tai Chi workouts can be facilitated through videos or DVDs and online instructions on YouTube- but do not lose sight of the most significant purpose of Tai Chi since this may not be fully explained in DVDs and videos. Success can only be achieved when you know the real purpose of Tai Chi.

Chapter 5: How to Find Serenity and Inner Peace through Tai Chi in 10 Steps

The purpose of Tai Chi is to establish harmony between the mind, body, spirit and Tao (universe). This is done by incorporating mind relaxation and breathing exercises into the different forms of Tai Chi. Remember to move slowly, but continuously and smoothly. Finding serenity and inner peace through Tai Chi can be done by following these steps:

Step #1 – Prepare yourself mentally

You have to prepare yourself mentally by openly welcoming the idea behind Tai Chi. Once you are mentally prepared, your whole body and spirit will respond positively as well. Empty your mind of any thoughts. Relax your body and mind.

Step #2 – Do the warm up exercises

Let our head roll around your neck several times. Stretch your arms and legs away from your body until they loosen up.

Step #3 – Perform the commencing form (the state of Wuji)

Stand normally and in a relaxed state with your arms hanging loosely at your sides. Your feet must be at least a foot apart and your back straight, yet relaxed. Inhale and exhale normally. Close your eyes, relax, and empty your mind of any thought. Stay that way until you are calm and at peace. This is performed before the complex steps are done.

Step #4 - Perform the opening Tai Chi form

Do this by standing with your feet at least shoulder-length apart and slightly pointing them inward. Allow your arms to hang at your sides, with the palms facing towards the back. Close your eyes and visualize a straight line from the middle of your head extending down to your feet. Inhale deeply and raise your arms slowly up to shoulder-level. Be aware of the air entering your lungs and instruct yourself mentally to relax. Remove all negative thoughts from your mind. Inhale, and slowly lower your arms to your sides. Do this several times until you feel your muscles relax.

Step #5 – Perform the simple Tao Chi exercises

Relax your muscles by performing the basic Tao Chi exercises given in Chapter 4. While doing these exercises, inhale and exhale. Notice how the air enters and leaves your body. Empty your mind of any thoughts. You can use the single whip position. Close your eyes to savor the exercise. Imagine your muscles releasing the tension and stress. Feel your muscles relax and grow stronger. There are hundreds of Tao Chi exercises used by practitioners, but for the short forms set, it is usually made up of 21 forms.

Step #6 – Maintain a state of mental calmness and peace

Maintain that state of calmness and peace while performing the exercise by savoring every movement and every breath that enters and leaves your body. Your mind must also be free of any negative thoughts. Your mental ability is crucial in this step. You can remain in this step for a few minutes until you have achieved this goal.

Step 7 – Reconnect with oneness

Imagine the Chi or energy of the whole universe around you, and you are a part of it. Imagine yourself as one of the branches or leaves in the vast tree that is our universe. You can perform quiet standing meditation while connecting to your oneness. Allow your body to relax and feel the energy flowing through you, calming you and bringing you inner peace. This can be difficult at first, especially if you are doing it alone. But with practice, you will eventually be able to do it easily.

Step #8 – You can proceed to the more advance Tai Chi forms

Once you have perfected the simple forms, you can proceed to practice the more complex forms such as "White horse shakes its mane" and "White crane spreads its wings."

Step #9 – Perform closure

This is done by standing with your feet apart and your hands cupped in front of your pelvic area. Inhale while slowly raising your cupped hands to shoulder level. Close your eyes and inhale. Visualize your hands cupping all the energy into your body bringing it to your chest. Then exhale, turning your fingers downward to "cup" the energy as you push down your fingers to your pelvic area.

Step #10 – Claim your serenity and inner peace

Do not get discouraged if all your anxieties and stress were not eliminated during your first try. That is natural. Most people do not achieve complete peace after their first exposure. Practice the Tao Chi exercises daily or even twice a day, and you will soon reap the superb benefits acquired from Tao Chi exercises.

The second to the 8th steps can be re-organized to suit your convenience. The end point is to attain peace and calm in mind, body and soul.

Chapter 6: Eighteen Important Tips for Practicing Tai Chi

Tai Chi encompasses broad forms of exercises created by many teachers. These tips include all forms of Tai Chi. These significant tips will help you as a beginner in adapting Tai Chi as one of your daily practices.

1. **Tai Chi is meditation while exercising.** Initially, you may not be able to execute both of these things simultaneously- but with practice, you will eventually succeed.

2. **Learning from a teacher can help facilitate the process.** If you know a certified teacher online or offline, you can join their group. Ensure that he is a qualified and competent professional before signing up.

3. **Persevere.** Never give up, and success will ultimately be yours. This is the mindset of most successful people.

4. **Choose the best Tai Chi form that suits your preferences.** You should enjoy the Tai Chi exercises you have selected in order for them to be effective.

5. **Learning Tai Chi is a challenge.** With the numerous number of forms, you may not be able learn all of them. Embarking on a new activity can be difficult at first, but patience is key. Perceive problems as challenges that can be successfully overcome.

6. **You can join Tai Chi classes.** To broaden your exposure, you can also enroll in online or offline Tai Chi classes. This will allow you to observe how other people perform the exercises, and learn from their mistakes.

7. **Do a daily Tai Chi.** No matter how many books and videos you have read and watched. You can never attain serenity and inner peace if you have not performed the Tai Chi exercises. Therefore, act on your plan.

8. **Set a regular time and place for your Tai Chi exercises.** This will allow you to be more organized and motivated to comply with your exercises.

9. **Spend at least 15 to 20 minutes to exercise.** Exercise daily and regularly for at least 15 to 20 minutes to ensure that the exercise and relaxation techniques have sunk into your system.

10. **Perform your workouts with smooth and continuous movements.** This is emphasized because it's one essential characteristic of the Tai Chi exercises.

11. **Memorize the sequence of your chosen moves.** For you to be able to move slowly but smoothly and fluidly, you have to memorize the moves that you have decided to use. This will allow you to move continuously without interruptions or kinks.

12. **Do added workouts even if you joined a class.** You'll need the extra workouts to adapt Tai Chi into your lifestyle. You'll have to do Tai Chi exercises permanently, if you want to achieve permanent inner peace and calm.

13. **Concentrate on your internal energy.** Tai Chi is not about brute force but is based on the strength of your internal energy. Therefore, when you do your exercises, summon your internal power and not your external strength.

14. **Take note that Tai Chi is also a form of martial arts.** It's not only a method to workout but you can use it effectively to ward of attackers too.

15. **It's fun joining groups.** Interacting with other people with the same interest can be fun and thrilling. Grab this chance to meet people who can motivate and encourage you more.

16. **Learn the fundamentals before the long forms.** Do this step-by-step. There is no need to rush. You have your entire lifetime to learn the more complex steps.

17. **There's no pain but with superb gains.** The cliché "No pain, no gain" is no longer applicable with Tai Chi exercises. You do not experience pain, yet you stand to gain a plethora of mental, spiritual and physical benefits.

18. **Tai Chi is safe and effective.** You do not need to worry. For a person without any serious illness, the workouts are safe and effective when properly implemented.

These are some general tips you should be aware of should you decide to join the growing number of Tai Chi enthusiasts all over the world. Be a smart learner, learn from your mistakes and from the mistakes of others- but do not be afraid to ask questions or to search for answers to those questions.

Conclusion

Having the desire to find serenity and inner peace by learning Tai Chi is commendable. You are brave enough to step forward and meet the challenge, although there is a chance you might not succeed. But as they say, you have not lost until you have given up trying.

Do not waste your time doing all the workouts you encounter. Instead, choose some workouts that are convenient for you and stick to them. After you have mastered them, that is the time you can move on to the other set of movements. Doing too many exercises is like stuffing your mouth with more food than you can chew. So choose properly and stick to your choices.

Remember that the workout is important, but what truly counts is your ability to harness your internal power and bring it to the fore. You can only do this when you are able to empty your mind and mentally position yourself for your internal energy to become evident.

Finding the harmony between mind, body, soul and the universe could be a gigantic task or a relatively easy one, depending on your frame of mind. If you believe you will succeed, you will. Allow me to incorporate this quotation about the power of a positive mind: "What the mind can conceive, the body can achieve."

Finally, I'd like to thank you for purchasing this book! If you enjoyed it or found it helpful, I'd greatly appreciate it if you'd take a moment to leave a review on Amazon. Thank you!

54945792R00027

Made in the USA
Lexington, KY
04 September 2016